As Big As

Suzannah Beddoes

Contents

Explorer Challenge
What animal is this?

OXFORD
UNIVERSITY PRESS

Look Back, Explorers

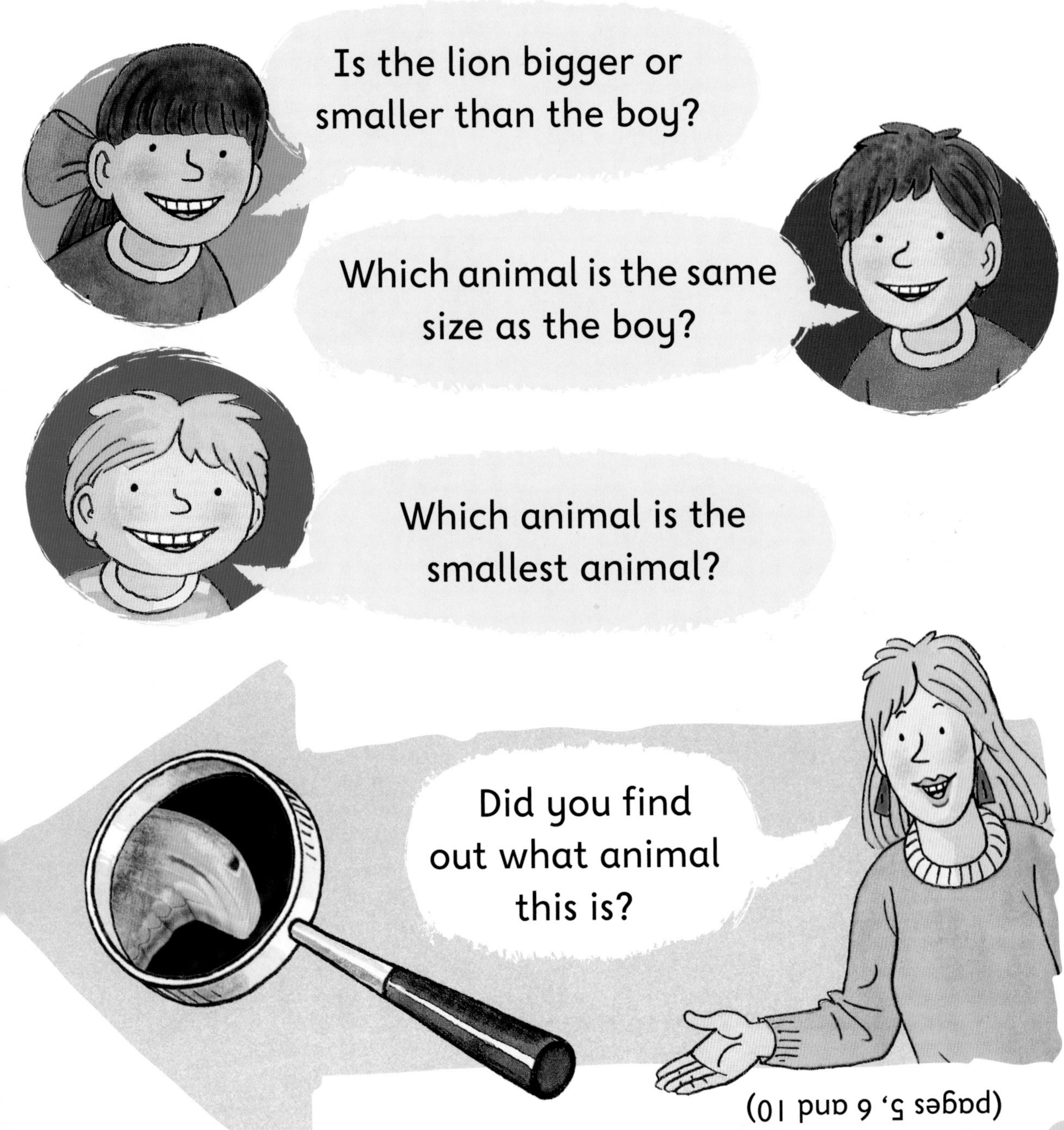

Is the lion bigger or smaller than the boy?
Which animal is the same size as the boy?
Which animal is the smallest animal?
Did you find out what animal this is?

Explorer Challenge: atlas moth (pages 5, 6 and 10)

What's Next, Explorers?

Now read about Kipper and Lee's big and small toys …

Explorer Challenge
for *Big!*

Which toy has these round ears?